The Greenwoods MULTIPLY and DiViDE Fractions

Brandy Crump

Illustrations by RKS Illustrations

ISBN: 978-1-7335296-2-4

[] + − × ÷ = ? ()

This book is dedicated to my baby that I miscarried in 2009. It was the pain of losing you that birthed this book series.

To my children, Myles and Bria, who inspire me to leave a legacy.

To Mr. Brown, former math teacher and coworker of 10 years, who kept asking me every single day, "Did you finish your books yet?" Well, Mr. Brown, I can finally say "YES!"

To Chris Nolen, former math teacher of 20 years and CEO of Nferno Productions, who read my manuscripts and said, "Hurry up and put those books out there!"

To the students who struggle in math and require simple explanations with examples of how it connects to their daily lives.

[] + − × ÷ = ? ()

[] + − × ÷ = ? ()

Mrs.Peterson, the fourth-grade teacher at Resilience Learning Academy, returned all of the graded work to her students. "OK class, now that you have your graded papers, I want you to correct your mistakes."Brea's grades on her papers were as follows: Adding/Subtracting Fractions, B+; Multiplying Fractions, A+; and Dividing Fractions, D–.

[] + − × ÷ = ? ()

[ ] + − × ÷ = ? ( )

Brea was very upset because this was the first time she earned a grade below B. She knew that her parents would be very disappointed if she did not improve her grade. As Mrs. Peterson passed out the last few papers, she asked if there were any questions. Brea raised her hand to get Mrs. Peterson's attention.

[ ] + − × ÷ = ? ( )

Mrs. Peterson walked over to Brea's desk. Brea asked, "Mrs. Peterson, why did I get a D– on dividing fractions?"

[ ] + − × ÷ = ? ( )

"Well Brea, take a look at the first problem and explain how you got the answer," replied Mrs. Peterson. The problem was:

$$\frac{2}{3} \div \frac{3}{4}$$

[ ] + − × ÷ = ? ( )

"First, I inverted or flipped the

$$\frac{2}{3},$$

making it

$$\frac{3}{2}.$$

[ ] + − ✕ ÷ = ? ( )

Next, I changed the division sign to multiplication and multiplied the numerators (top numbers) to get 9 and multiplied the denominators (bottom numbers) to get 8. You told us to invert one of the fractions and then multiply straight across, so why did I get this wrong?" Brea asked.

[ ] + − ✕ ÷ = ? ( )

[] + − × ÷ = ? ()

"Brea, you had the right idea of inverting one of the fractions but you must remember the following phrase:"

KEEP, CHANGE, AND FLIP

[] + − × ÷ = ? ()

[] + − × ÷ = ? ()

"Now say it with me, Brea," requested Mrs. Peterson.

"KEEP, CHANGE, AND FLIP," said the duo. "Brea, now write it down in your notebook," Mrs. Peterson said. Brea proceeded to record the statement KEEP, CHANGE, AND FLIP in her math notebook.

[] + − × ÷ = ? ()

[ ] **+** **—** **✕** **÷** **=** **?** ( )

"Brea, when dividing fractions, we will KEEP the first fraction the same, CHANGE the division symbol to multiplication, FLIP (invert) the second fraction, and then multiply the fractions straight across," said Mrs. Peterson.

[ ] **+** **—** **✕** **÷** **=** **?** ( )

[ ] + − × ÷ = ? ( )

"Now, redo the problem using the KEEP, CHANGE, FLIP METHOD, and then defend your new answer," Mrs. Peterson requested.

[ ] + − × ÷ = ? ( )

Brea erased the incorrect steps and then wrote the following:

$$\frac{2}{3} \div \frac{3}{4}$$

$$= \frac{2}{3} \times \frac{4}{3}$$

$$= \frac{8}{9}$$

"Mrs. Peterson, I kept the first fraction

$$\frac{2}{3}$$

the same, changed the division sign to multiplication, flipped (inverted) the second fraction to get

$$\frac{4}{3}$$

[ ] + − ✕ ÷ = ? ( )

and then multiplied the fractions straight across to get

$$\frac{8}{9}$$

as my final answer," said Brea. "Great job, Brea! Now you are ready to correct the rest of your work. Call me when you are done, OK?" Mrs. Peterson said.

[ ] + − ✕ ÷ = ? ( )

[ ] + − × ÷ = ? ( )

Brea proceeded to erase the incorrect work beneath the next problem, which was

$$\frac{3}{5} \div \frac{1}{2}.$$

[ ] + − × ÷ = ? ( )

She wrote
the following:

$$\frac{3}{5} \div \frac{1}{2}$$

[ ] + − ✕ ÷ = ? ( )

$$= \frac{3}{5} \times \frac{2}{1}$$

$$= \frac{6}{5}$$

Before proceeding to the third problem, Brea checked her steps to the second problem. In her head she said, "I kept

$$\frac{3}{5}$$

[ ] + − ✕ ÷ = ? ( )

[] + – × ÷ = ? ()

the same, changed the division sign to multiplication, and then flipped (inverted)

$$\frac{1}{2}$$ changing it to $$\frac{2}{1}.$$

Next, I multiplied straight across to get

$$\frac{6}{5}$$

as my final answer."

[] + – × ÷ = ? ()

[ ] + − × ÷ = ? ( )

When Brea was done correcting her worksheet, she motioned for Mrs. Peterson to come check her answers. Mrs. Peterson was very pleased with Brea's work and changed her grade on dividing fractions from a D− to an A+.

Brea's parents were proud when they saw her grades at the end of the week. She had the following grades: Adding and Subtracting Fractions, A+; Multiplying Fractions, A+; and Dividing Fractions, A+.

[ ] + − × ÷ = ? ( )

[ ] + − × ÷ = ? ( )

Brandy Crump is the author of a math book series which includes the following titles: (1) The Greenwoods Add and Subtract Fractions with Like Denominators, (2) The Greenwoods Add and Subtract Fractions with Unlike Denominators, (3) The Greenwoods Multiply and Divide Fractions, (4) The Greenwoods Simplify Percents, (5) The Greenwoods Add and Subtract Integers, (6) The Greenwoods Solve One-Step Equations, and (7) The Greenwoods Solve Proportions. Brandy holds a bachelor's degree in Secondary Math Education and a master's degree in Educational Administration. She has 18 years of experience in teaching mathematics to at-risk students who suffer from adverse childhood experiences (ACES). She grew up in Harvey, Illinois, and graduated from Thornton Township High School where she taught for 14 years. As the product of an underserved, poverty-stricken, and high-crime community, she experienced ACES that prepared her to better understand and connect with her delinquent and at-risk students. She has provided workshops on effective classroom management through mutually respectful relationships and increasing student engagement through cooperative groups and authentic learning activities. Brandy is a lifelong learner and continues to research best practices for reaching out to struggling students. She is a member of Delta Sigma Theta Sorority Incorporated. She enjoys working with the youth in her community, writing books, creating math games, and conducting motivational speaking engagements.

[ ] + − × ÷ = ? ( )

www.ingramcontent.com/pod-product-compliance
Lightning Source LLC
LaVergne TN
LVHW072102070426
835508LV00002B/235